HeyZeus

A modern mystery drama

by Frank Thomas Smith

Frank Thomas Smith
Author/Playwright

Celina MacKern
Illustrator

ISBN: 9781476302760 paperback
9781948302777 eBook

James D. Stewart
Editor

HeyZeus

First Printing Copyright © August 2025 by
Anthroposophical Publications
https://AnthroposophicalPubllications.org/

All rights reserved. No part of this drama may be reproduced in any form or by any electronic or mechanical means including information storage and retrieval systems, without permission in writing from the author and/or the publisher. The only exception is by a reviewer, who may quote short excerpts in a review.

This drama is a work of fiction. Names, characters, places, and incidents either are products of the author's imagination or are used fictitiously. Any resemblance to actual persons, living or dead, events, or locales is entirely coincidental.

Cast of Characters

THOMAS PAULSON: The protagonist, an advertising executive grappling with faith and purpose after encountering HeyZeus.

MARY HEALY: Widow of the deceased Harry, reflecting on her troubled marriage.

LARRY HEALY: Brother of the deceased, a humorous and nostalgic figure.

MR. HEALY: Father of the deceased, opinionated and resistant to change.

JUDY: Thomas' girlfriend, a young black actress who challenges his beliefs and decisions.

DR. EISBEIN: A psychiatrist who analyzes Thomas' experience with HeyZeus.

CHAIRMAN OF THE BOARD (C.B.): Owner of the advertising agency, focused on profit and dismissive of moral concerns.

MARGO: Thomas' ex-wife, a savvy businesswoman who secures major accounts for the agency.

JOHN: A cynical employee at the advertising agency where Thomas works.

BISHOP CASEY: A Catholic bishop who dismisses Thomas' claims about HeyZeus.

MAGDALENA: A punk-styled young woman who believes in HeyZeus and delivers his message.

FIRST MAN: A passerby in Prospect Park, a skeptical and blunt fellow.

ICE AGENT: A former Catholic priest turned immigration officer, suspicious of HeyZeus.

OFFICER PILATUS: A police officer involved in the tragic shooting of HeyZeus.

Each character contributes to the play's exploration of faith, societal issues, and human connection.

Table of Contents

HEYZEUS 1
CAST OF CHARACTERS 3
ACT ONE 7
   SCENE ONE 7
      PROSPECT PARK 7
   SCENE TWO 14
      THE WAKE 14
   SCENE THREE 30
      THE GIRLFRIEND 30
ACT TWO 47
   SCENE ONE 47
      THE SHRINK 47
   SCENE TWO 65
      TRUE ADVERTISING 65
   SCENE THREE 81
      THE BISHOP 81
ACT THREE 99
   SCENE ONE 99
      PROSPECT PARK REDUX 99
   SCENE TWO 123
      A SPECIAL LOVE 123
MUSICAL SUGGESTIONS 131
ON-LINE ACTIVITIES 133
ABOUT THE PLAYWRIGHT 135
OTHER BOOKS 137

ACT ONE

SCENE ONE

PROSPECT PARK

Setting: Park bench left of center.

At Rise: Spring, the stage is in darkness when the introductory music begins. A spot shines on THOMAS, standing downstage a few paces right of center. As he speaks, the light gradually expands to reveal the park bench.

THOMAS

(To the audience)

I invited you here today in order to tell you about something extraordinary that happened to me recently here in Prospect Park. Thomas Wolfe wrote that "Only the dead know Brooklyn". Maybe that's why it still has a bad reputation. Partly it's deserved of course, but not entirely. There are parts of Brooklyn that don't deserve a bad reputation. Brooklyn is very big you know, and that's a reason why it's so hard to know it. And it's only one borough of New York City, which is bigger than some countries. Actually New York City [*Wry grin*] should secede from the United States and Brooklyn could then be a state, or province ... don't you think? And it could be divided into its original natural neighborhoods: Flatbush, Greenpoint, Williamsburg, Bedford-Stuyvesant, Bay Ridge, Canarsie, Crown Heights, and the rest. Aren't they beautiful names? What's in a name? "A rose by any other name would smell as sweet." I don't agree. I mean ... a name is symbolic and if something has a beautiful name it tends to become like its name, eventually ... maybe. [*Smiles*] Or maybe not. Prospect Park is in Flatbush, which seems like an unlikely place for this kind of encounter, I admit that. One would expect it to happen on a road to somewhere, like Damascus. But a road could also be a path, like this one [*Points behind him*]. Although the place could be anywhere ... it seems.

I don't live in Brooklyn anymore, although I was born and grew up here a long time ago, until I left to go to college, the University of Vermont, of all places. Whew! Then I came home for a while, then left again pretty definitely. But that's not really relevant. [*Looks down at the ground for a few moments, thinking, then looks up again*] So I'll get to the point. I live in New Jersey now, across the river, there [*points*], and work in Manhattan. I received the news that a close friend had died here in Brooklyn, so I came over on a Saturday, like this one, to attend his wake in a funeral parlor nearby. If you know anything about Irish wakes – Brooklyn ones at least – you'll know that they're not as depressing as they should be. You meet a lot of old friends and after crossing yourself [*Makes the sign of the cross*] in front of the coffin and kissing the deceased's relatives, you slouch over to the bar next door to have a drink, or more than one. There's always a bar next door to Irish-oriented funeral parlors, by the way. But instead of going directly to the funeral parlor, I came to the park. It was the first time I'd been here in a long time. I didn't have a conscious motive, I guess I just wanted some air to fortify myself for the sickly-sweet ordeal of the wake. It was summer. [*He takes off his jacket*] I came to this bench and sat down. The lake in front of me [*Motions*]. And the ducks [*Sound of ducks quacking*]. I recalled Holden Caulfield's question: what happens to the ducks in the park in winter? He meant Central Park over in Manhattan, but the principle's the same. I realized that I still didn't know the answer. That was my train of thought when he came along. [*Looks right*] He was about my age, maybe a bit younger, wore jeans and a blue T-shirt and sneakers. And he was black. He looked like a guy out for a stroll on Saturday afternoon. Oh, and with his hands in his pockets; I remember it exactly. He stopped in front of me, looked at the lake and said, "I bet you're wondering where those ducks go in winter when the lake freezes over." Then he turned and smiled at me, a beautiful smile. You can imagine that I was nonplussed. I said, Yeah, I was wondering that. Maybe their wings are clipped so they can't fly far and then they're rounded up and taken somewhere for the winter. He shook his head and said, "No, actually some fly south, and others stay here, huddled together out of the water to keep warm. They keep pretty well hidden." I stood up. [*He stands and faces the audience*] We were about the same height.

Now comes the part kind of hard to explain. [*Pause*] I had the strangest feeling about him. It was almost like falling in love with someone at first sight. There was simply something about that guy that was lovable. So naturally I didn't want him to leave. I asked him if he'd like to sit down, and he said he'd like to show me something first. Then, suddenly, a strong, cold wind arose. It was strange, something like that happening in Spring. A really strong cold wind whipped up out of nowhere and it became dark; it was like an eclipse of the sun. And that guy walks, casually, over to the edge of the lake. [*goes to the edge of the stage*] And keeps walking! ... onto the water, not *in*to it but *on*to it. The ripples ... not waves ... just ripples in the water were alive, as though some great fish was beneath the surface furiously thrashing its tail. I know it sounds crazy, and you can believe me or not, but that's what he did: walk on the water. About fifteen paces, then turns around and comes back.

Now I wasn't born yesterday, far from it, and I know that there are con artists around who can make you believe they can bend spoons with their minds and stuff like that. So, I tried to be skeptical at first. When he sat down next to me, dry as one of Healy's martini's, I said to him, "Hey, who are you, anyway?" He answered, "My name is HeyZeus, Thomas." I thought he was a Puerto Rican or something like that, so I asked him what country he was from. No one is called Jesus in America, it sounds funny, but in places like Puerto Rico or Mexico it's common. "No,

Thomas, not Jesús with an s and an accent on the u. Just HeyZeus, with a Z, and I'm from Brooklyn." He picked up a twig, bent down and wrote with it on the ground. "Greek, huh?" I asked. He just smiled.

As you can imagine, a lot of things were going through my head, like if he was Jesus, or HeyZeus, whatever, how come he's black? Telling it now, it's ... I mean it sounds weird, But you know, I have to admit it ... I already believed him. That may seem naive to you, but you weren't there. I assure you that I'm not the kind of guy who goes around believing all kinds of fake shit without proof. I'm not gullible, not even religious. On the contrary, I was pretty much an agnostic before I met him, had even been analyzed once by a Freudian shrink. But I believed him anyway. (pause) Still do. Sure, I asked myself: why me? If Jesus Christ – or HeyZeus as he calls himself now – is going to appear to somebody, why me? Why not the Pope or some saint, or Bishop Casey, for example?

"Why *not* you, Thomas?" he asked me. "Because there must be plenty of others who would be more appropriate," I answered, getting used to having my mind read. "That isn't for you to judge," he said. Not much I could say to that, was there? [*Pause*] You know, it wasn't so much his walking on the water that convinced me. It was ... *him, his presence.* [*Pause*] Do you see? [*Pause*] I guess not. We sat for a while, and it was beautiful just to be able to sit next to him like that. But when it became obvious that he wasn't going to contribute much to the conversation, at least not in the line of small talk, I felt I was expected to ask him something, so I did. I didn't call him master or rabbi or even sir. That's not my style. Besides, he didn't look like any of those. I just asked him now that he's here again – on earth that is – what are his plans? He looked at me – his eyes were very penetrating, that's what I mostly remember about them – and said, "I could ask you the same thing." "Me?" I said stupidly. "Yes, what are your plans, Thomas?" Well, the fact is I had no plans, except going to the wake ... so, after appearing to mull it over, I asked him what he expected me to do. What he said next shows that he has a sense of humor, which doesn't come out much in the Bible. He shrugged and said he'd have to give me the usual answer, like I should know what it is. But I didn't know so I asked him. "Follow me!" he said. [*Long pause*] I asked him if he meant literally and he said, "Look it up. And draw your own conclusion. Do what you think best. It's all up to you. Times have changed and I can't go around telling you what to do anymore, even if you ask." Then he said he must be getting along, slaps his knees [*Demonstrates*] and stands up. [*Stands*] I was thinking I'd like to touch him, just to make sure he's real, but didn't know how to go about it. I couldn't very well shake his hand and say it was great meeting you, HeyZeus. Naturally he knew what I was thinking and when I stood up, he kissed me on the cheek. [*Touches his cheek with two fingers*] Then he strolled away in the direction from which he had come. [*Looks left*] hands in pockets, humming, yes, humming one of those old Beatles ballads: *Let it be.* When he disappeared around the bend of the path, I stood there for a while, then started walking around, because I felt nervous. I guess you can understand that. [*Walks around*] I didn't follow him because I had to go to the wake. Somehow, I knew that's what he wanted me to do. Then I went, almost ran, to the funeral parlor. I wanted to tell someone. Larry and Mary Healy were there when I arrived.

[**BLACKOUT**]

SCENE TWO

THE WAKE

Setting: In dim light LARRY and Mr. HEALY enter carrying a coffin. They set it on two A-frames or other simple device downstage right. They exit and return with two long candle holders and candles, which they place at both ends of the coffin. One of them lights the candles. [*They exit*] LARRY returns carrying two chairs, which he places upstage center, facing the coffin. He approaches the coffin, opens it, makes the sign of the cross, silently says a prayer. MARY enters and sits on one of the chairs. She is dressed in black. LARRY crosses himself again, kisses his thumb and sits in the other chair. [*Lights up, but not full*]

LARRY:

Do you remember the time Harry got stinking drunk at the Breezy Point Surf Club and fell out of the window of the Blarney Stone bar into the ocean?

MARY:

Harry was always good for a laugh.

LARRY:

I suspected that he fell out of that window on purpose, for the laugh.

MARY:

He could have killed himself, but it would have been worth it.

LARRY:

That wouldn't exactly have been a laugh.

MARY:

It would have been a sensation though, and that interested him even more than a laugh. What a way to go, his drunken friends would have said admiringly.

LARRY:

Better than cirrhosis of the liver.

MARY:

That wasn't very sensational, was it?

LARRY:

But inevitable. [*Pause*] Not many of the old crowd around anymore. I've lost track of most of them.

MARY:

The ones who came to the wake didn't stay long. They're next door getting a load on, along with Harry's family.

LARRY:

Any sign of Tom Paulson?

MARY:

Not yet. Since he became a big shot in the advertising business he has no time for his old friends, or a grieving widow.

LARRY:

He might come after all. Dad called him and he said he'd come. You and he were going steady when Harry was falling out of windows. I thought you two were stuck on each other for keeps.

MARY:

So did I.

LARRY:

You two made a great couple. The basketball star and the prettiest girl on the block.

MARY:

And his cheer leader.

LARRY:

Yeah, and that. Whatever broke it up? You never told me.

MARY:

I don't really know. He went away to college. At first, he wrote long letters describing every move he made. He loved and missed me *so* much. Then the letters got shorter and less frequent until they stopped altogether. He didn't come home for Easter vacation, said he had to study. So I went up there, all the way to Vermont. God, what a desolate place, all mountains and trees and hick towns. Tom was mixed up in some wacky agriculture project in a place called High Mowing or Low Mowing, Biodynamic, something like that, supposed to be spiritual. Said he had to go there, that it was very important. More important than me, obviously. He was mad that I went up there without asking him first. It wasn't pleasant. He was so obviously trying to get rid of me that I left after one day.

LARRY:

Another woman?

MARY:

I suppose. Isn't it always?

LARRY:

That's what they say.

MARY:

So Harry caught me on the rebound. I made him promise to go on the wagon.

LARRY:

If he did it didn't last long.

MARY:

When we got married he said he'd give it up forever, for me. But I should have known that someone like Harry doesn't give up his booze for a mere wife.

LARRY:

I doubt he could have even if he wanted to. Sorry to say it Mary, but I think he's better off out of his misery.

MARY:

We both are, so don't be sorry.

[*Enter THOMAS, out of breath*]

LARRY:

Hey! Speak of the devil. Hi, Tommy.

THOMAS:

[*Surprised*] Larry! But I thought … [*Goes to coffin and looks in*] Oh! [*Laughs shortly, becomes serious, makes the sign of the cross, stands awkwardly in front of the coffin for a few seconds, goes to Larry, shakes his hand*] Am I glad to see you!

LARRY:

Likewise, but what's going on?

THOMAS:

It was a misunderstanding. I thought your father said *you* died. He must have said Harry, but I understood Larry.

MARY:

Harry's last laugh.

LARRY:

Yeah, he sure would have gotten a kick out of it. [*Looks at coffin*]

THOMAS:

I'm sorry, Mary. [*Kisses her on the cheek*]

MARY:

I bet you're relieved it's him instead of your friend Larry. I can't say I blame you.

THOMAS:

[*After an embarrassed pause*] What a day! You know, I went to Prospect Park before coming here and …

MARY:

We were wondering if you'd come.

THOMAS:

I just wanted to get some fresh air, but the damnedest thing happened …

[*Enter MR HEALY*]

MR. HEALY:

[*To THOMAS*] Hello, hooker. Long time no see.

THOMAS:

Hello Mr. Healy. How are you?

MR. HEALY:

Not bad, considering. Where've you been keeping yourself?

THOMAS:

I've been very busy lately. I live in New Jersey now.

MR. HEALY:

It's very good of you to come all this way for Harry's sake.

THOMAS:

I'm very sorry for your loss, sir.

MR. HEALY:

Thank you. Harry was a ... er ... free spirit.

[*An embarrassed silence follows, broken by MARY*]

MARY:

If he'd known it was Harry, he probably wouldn't have come.

MR. HEALY:

What do you mean?

LARRY:

Tommy thought it was me in there. [*Points to the coffin*] A case of mistaken identity.

MR. HEALY:

But I told you ... oh, I get it – Harry/Larry. [*Laughs*]

MARY:

[*To coffin*] Looks like the joke's on you, lover.

MR. HEALY:

[*To THOMAS*] I heard you finally got married.

THOMAS:

Some time ago.

MARY:

How's your wife?

THOMAS:

Fine.

LARRY:

Why don't you bring her around sometime?

THOMAS:

I can't afford it. She invested in a good lawyer and squeezed the maximum alimony out of me.

MR. HEALY:

That didn't last very long. Was she Catholic?

THOMAS:

She *is* Protestant, more or less.

Mr. HEALY:

Were you married in the Church?

THOMAS:

Justice of the Peace, Staten Island.

MR. HEALY:

So you weren't married at all in the eyes of the Church.

MARY:

What luck!

LARRY:

Hey, now you two can pick up where you left off.

MARY:

Lawrence!

MR. HEALY:

Harry's not even in the grave yet, Larry. So you really

should be more respectful. [*Pause*] If you ask me, though, it's not a bad idea. You two made such a beautiful couple.

MARY:

Nobody asked you.

MR. HEALY:

It's not the first time I've spouted off without being asked. Any offspring, Thomas?

THOMAS:

No. I was going to say that the damnedest thing happened in the park …

MR. HEALY:

Harry beat you there. Two lovely children.

THOMAS:

I didn't know. Is there insurance?

MARY:

There is, but we aren't allowed to use it in this parish.

THOMAS:

I meant …

MARY:

I know what you meant. Yes, Harry sold the stuff, so he made sure he had enough himself. I think he was his own best customer.

THOMAS:

You seem bitter, Mary.

MARY:

I have reason to be. What were you going to say about the park?

THOMAS:

Yes. I was standing near the lake when a guy came along. Nothing special looking about him. Youngish, black, wearing jeans and a T-shirt ...

MR. HEALY:

In this neighborhood you're lucky if you see a white man anymore.

LARRY:

You can say that again.

MR. HEALY:

In this neighborhood you're lucky if you see a white man anymore.

LARRY:

Ha ha. Hey, did you hear the story about the Irish cab driver who had an accident? A Cadillac bumped into him near the UN, so he gets out of his taxi and goes over to the Cadi and this big black guy is in the back seat. He starts to yell at the driver, but the black guy gets out and yells at him that he's the Guinean ambassador. That's in Africa somewhere. So the Irishman hauls off and socks him one. Finally the cops come and take him to jail. You know what he tells the judge? I knew that colored guy was a phony as soon as he said he was a Guinea. I know an Eye-talian when I see one. [*All laugh except THOMAS*]

MR. HEALY:

That's a good one. Although it's so old it's got whiskers.

LARRY:

It's supposed to be true.

MARY:

Why not? Only an Irishman could be that dumb.

LARRY:

You never see suntans next door, Dad. How do you manage to keep them out.

MR. HEALY:

I ignore them as long as I can. Then I give them the eye. [*Demonstrates, LARRY laughs*] Then I give them the old silent treatment; they get the message.

LARRY:

I gotta hand it to you; Healy's Bar and Grill is an oasis in a fucking jungle. Sorry Mary.

MARY:

I have nothing against them as such. I'm only afraid for my children.

MR. HEALY:

Goddamn right you are. Not even the Catholic schools are safe anymore. You were smart to get out when you did, Tom. If I don't keep them out my white customers won't come in anymore. Although most of them are moving away anyway. I'm looking for another place in Queens but keep it to yourselves.

LARRY:

Queens isn't much better than here. Out on Long Island would be better.

MR. HEALY:

I know, but I mean how far can you go? They multiply like jackrabbits. Soon even the Island will be overrun. And now to add insult to injury we got the Porto Ricans.

LARRY:

You can't even tell what color they are half the time.

MR. HEALY:

They come in all shades. It's the same difference. [*Pause, looks at THOMAS*] So what about that guy in the park; was he the Porto Rican ambassador, or what?

THOMAS:

Something like that.

MARY:

What do you mean.

THOMAS:

He's an ambassador without portfolio.

MR. HEALY:

What's that supposed to mean.

THOMAS:

Do you know what he did? He walked on the lake.

LARRY:

On the lake?

MARY:

Have you been drinking, Tommy?

THOMAS:

Who do you know who walked on the water, Mary?

MR. HEALY:

Do you mean to say that Porto Rican walked on the water like Jesus Christ? What circus is he from?

LARRY:

Let him finish.

MR. HEALY:

OK, go ahead. But I gotta warn you Tom: I don't like religious jokes if they're dirty.

THOMAS:

It's not a joke. I'm dead serious. He walked *on* the lake. He told me his name is HeyZeus. That sounds like Jesus in Spanish.

MR. HEALY:

So, what are you tryin' to tell us, that Jesus is a darky? Come off it, Tom. I don't like your sense of humor.

THOMAS:

And I don't like your arrogance and racism.

LARRY:

You can call it arrogance if you like, but this is a free country and you can like or not like, whatever you want.

MR. HEALY:

You can kiss their asses for all I care, but don't go comparing them to our Lord.

THOMAS:

[*Furiously*] And what are you gonna do about it if I do?

MARY:

Don't be like that, Tom. I know how you feel, but you gotta understand how we feel too. The neighborhood's changed a lot since they started moving in and …

THOMAS:

OK Mary, save it. I know the whole story and I'm sick of hearing it. I'm not asking you to believe anything. I'm just telling you what I saw and what I felt and you can take it or leave it. So you leave it. Fine, that's OK with me.

MR. HEALY:

You're goddamn right we leave it.

MARY:

Can't we change the subject? It's terrible fighting like this after not having seen each other for such a long time.

LARRY:

Yeah, you're right. Let's change the subject. Playing any ball lately, Tommy?

THOMAS:

[*Pause*] Why no, not for years.

LARRY:

Too bad, you were good, potential pro, except kinda short for that.

MR. HEALY:

Goddamn Zulus dominate the sport nowadays anyway. A normal white man don't stand a chance.

LARRY:

Oh, I don't know about that.

THOMAS:

[*Looks at his watch*] Ah ... I gotta be going now. [*Slowly backs toward the exit*]

LARRY:

Aren't you coming next door for a quick one? Come on, it's on me.

MR. HEALY:

It's on the house.

THOMAS:

No, really, it's later than I thought.

MR. HEALY:

Well, it's been great seeing you again, son.

LARRY:

Don't be such a stranger.

MARY:

Goodbye Tom.

THOMAS:

Goodbye Mary. Be seeing you guys. [*Exits*]

LARRY:

He's changed a lot, if you ask me.

MR. HEALY:

Porto Ricans ain't got no ambassador. They're Americans, unfortunately.

LARRY:

[*To MARY*] He still likes you, Sis. I could tell. You should have given him your phone number.

MARY:

He can look it up … if he wants. Let's go get that drink on the house. [walks slowly to the coffin and blows out one of the candles.]

[**BLACKOUT**, *except for the other candle*]

SCENE THREE

THE GIRLFRIEND

Setting: Dim lights, soft music. THOMAS prepares the set: a table downstage center, a chair on either side, a half-empty bottle of red wine and two glasses. JUDY enters with a candle, which she places on the table and lights. THOMAS pours wine into the glasses. They sit. [*Lights up, soft.*]

JUDY:

So, what now? I mean it's all very interesting, but so what?

THOMAS:

So plenty. If Jesus Christ himself appears to you in Prospect Park, it must mean *some*thing for god's sake.

JUDY:

What? ... assuming it was him.

THOMAS:

That's what I'm trying to figure out.

JUDY:

Is that why you disappeared without telling anyone, especially me?

THOMAS:

Yes, I had to get away by myself and think.

JUDY:

Where did you go?

THOMAS:

Oh, for god's sake, Judy, what difference does that make?

JUDY:

Just asking. I'm interested in you, you know.

THOMAS:

Sorry. [*Pause*] I went to Italy.

JUDY:

Italy! Tom, you *know* I always wanted to go to Italy!

THOMAS:

I had to go alone, Judy. Don't you understand that? I might just as well have gone to Coney Island. It doesn't matter where I went. I took a taxi to the airport and got on the first plane going somewhere and it happened to be Italy.

JUDY:

You don't take an airplane to Coney Island. [*Pause*] Where in Italy?

THOMAS:

Como, near Milan.

JUDY:

Why there?

THOMAS:

The flight went to Milan and I didn't feel like staying in the city, so I asked in the tourist office where's a nice place not too far away.

JUDY:

Was it nice?

THOMAS:

Very. It's on a huge lake – Lake Como – spotted with villas. Even Mussolini had a villa there. A lot of churches. Italy has beautiful churches. You can tell they meant it when they were building their churches.

JUDY:

What did you do besides go to church?

THOMAS:

I didn't go to church. I only looked at them. I took a room in a small hotel on a mountain – a hill really – and walked around and thought a lot. You remember that my grandmother was Italian, and I learned some Italian from her when I was a kid. So I tried practicing it a little.

JUDY:

Who with?

THOMAS:

[*Exasperated*] The innkeeper's daughter, dark-tressed and plump. I slept with her every night.

JUDY:

I wouldn't doubt it. [*Pause*] Was all that thinking worthwhile?

THOMAS:

I decided he must want me to do something.

JUDY:

Did he *tell* you he wanted you to do something?

THOMAS:

I already told you, no. He left it up to me. He said I should follow him, but he didn't mean I should, you know, follow him at that moment.

JUDY:

Why not? How do you know?

THOMAS:

From the way he said it. He said look it up. Some things have to be modified, I guess. I mean things have changed a lot since then.

JUDY:

Since when?

THOMAS:

Since the first time he came, like it says in the Bible. He said to look it up, and where else could I look? I figure the message must be basically the same, although it's not easy to determine what the message is. There are a lot of contradictions. But what the hell, real life is full of contradictions. But whatever the message is, we seem to be doing the opposite.

JUDY:

Which is not surprising, given the state of things.

THOMAS:

We make the state of things.

JUDY:

So he leaves a message and retires to a fleecy cloud for a couple thousand years or so.

THOMAS:

But he left in the most dramatic way. You, as an actress, should be the first to realize that.

JUDY:

That script was written by others, way after the events. Who knows to what extent they used their creative imaginations. Anyway, we're not in a theater striving for dramatic effects.

THOMAS:

If I tell people about what happened in the park, it could have a dramatic effect, I mean, on reality.

JUDY:

It sure could. They'll say you're crazy.

THOMAS:

Do you think I'm crazy?

JUDY:

I didn't say that. But other people will.

THOMAS:

If you don't think I'm crazy or lying, you must believe me.

JUDY:

I didn't say that either.

THOMAS:

What then? It must be one or the other.

JUDY:

Why? It could have been a dream. That doesn't make you crazy.

THOMAS:

It wasn't a dream. I know the difference between dreaming and waking.

JUDY:

I don't understand you, Tommy. People don't walk on water …

THOMAS:

Jesus did.

JUDY:

… anymore. Besides, who knows if he really did, even then?

THOMAS:

Look it up.

JUDY:

Who believes that stuff nowadays? Least of all you … until now. What's happened to you?

THOMAS:

I just finished telling you what happened to me. When

you see something with your own eyes you can't help but believe it.

JUDY:

That depends on what it is.

THOMAS:

Judy ... ah ... you know, there are going to be some changes.

JUDY:

In what?

THOMAS:

In us, actually. I mean ... [*Trails off*]

JUDY:

Tell me, Tom.

THOMAS:

Our marriage plans. I've got this on my mind and can hardly think of anything else. So I don't think this is the right time for it. I mean ... you understand, don't you?

JUDY:

No, frankly I don't. Next you'll want to give up sex.

THOMAS:

You mean celibacy?

JUDY:

You *are* thinking of it.

THOMAS:

You brought it up.

JUDY:

God, you might as well tell me you've caught leprosy, that wouldn't be as bad. I don't know why you didn't become a priest instead of an ad man.

THOMAS:

My guardian angel saved me from going to a Jesuit school – Brooklyn Prep? - or I might have.

JUDY:

Good for him. How'd he manage it?

THOMAS:

He must have numbed my brain; I failed the entrance exam.

JUDY:

Look, Tommy, I'm a perfectly healthy, hardworking, emancipated – in quotation marks – actress. And I *need* sex, regularly and in healthy doses. I've been listening to all this shit patiently, but now you're going too far. Do you know what Erika would say? I can hear her now: Wow, I've heard some creative excuses to get out of a marriage, but this one takes the cake.

THOMAS:

Oh, come on, Judy.

JUDY:

I mean it, Tom, you can take your choice.

THOMAS:

You or him?

JUDY:

[*Long pause*] Tommy, we have a problem. And I think we need help.

THOMAS:

What kind of help?

JUDY:

Professional help.

THOMAS:

We?

JUDY:

OK you, but it's our problem, darling.

THOMAS:

Been there, done that.

JUDY:

What do you mean?

THOMAS:

Shrink stuff.

JUDY:

It didn't seem to help much.

THOMAS:

There was nothing to help.

JUDY:

Why did you do it then?

THOMAS:

A woman talked me into it. Guess who.

JUDY:

Your dear ex-wife, I bet.

THOMAS:

She meant well.

JUDY:

She must have had a reason to want you to go into analysis.

THOMAS:

She said I was impotent.

JUDY:

[*Laughs*] You – impotent? It must have worked after all. [*Pause*] Were you?

THOMAS:

Did you ever hear of female impotence?

JUDY:

Frankly, no.

THOMAS:

It exists though; it's what makes men impotent. Women are only the carriers.

JUDY:

Impotence is psychological.

THOMAS:

Yeah, well the analysis wasn't completely unsuccessful. I even began to believe some of it on the shrink's authority – at least my brain did, along with my genitals. The only part of me that resisted was my heart.

JUDY:

The heart is not the best organ to think with.

THOMAS:

I'm not so sure of that. In its way the heart thinks too. Only it's harder to get the message. Too much static from the nerve center.

JUDY:

Tommy, if I ask you to do it for me ... I don't mean to go into analysis again. Just see someone – a professional who could listen to your story. I mean, you know, about Zeus ...

THOMAS:

HeyZeus!

JUDY:

HeyZeus ... maybe give you some kind of test to see if your mental judgment is kinda, I don't know, like in order. [*Pause*] Please Tommy, think of me. Suddenly, out of a clear blue sky, you tell me that everything's changed. [*Pause*] You don't say that you don't love me, although you haven't said that you still do either …

THOMAS:

[*Interrupting*] I do, Judy, I do!

JUDY:

All the more reason to check up on yourself. Perhaps unconsciously you're afraid to marry me and all this is an elaborate scheme by your unconscious mind to relieve you of the guilt. In this way you transfer the responsibility to someone else – to this HeyZeus. Do you see what I mean?

THOMAS:

[*Dejectedly*] Yes. Have you discussed this with anyone already?

JUDY:

No! I swear! Will you do it then, for me? I can find the name of someone good. That's no problem.

THOMAS:

And if I say no?

JUDY:

It would mean that you no longer care, that you don't love me, and … well … it would mean, for me, that it's over, Tom … oh, Tommy.

THOMAS:

O.K. I'll do it.

JUDY:

Oh Tommy, I knew you'd be reasonable. I just know that everything will work itself out. [*Cheerfully*] How about some music? [*Goes off to turn on music, returns immediately, lifts glass*] Cheers, darling.

THOMAS:

Salute.

JUDY:

Let's dance. [*They dance, until the music slows and she melts into his arms*] Tommy?

THOMAS:

Yes?

JUDY:

I'm so glad I don't have female impotence. Aren't you?

THOMAS:

Yes, my love, very glad.

JUDY:

Darling? About the wedding. Is it still on, same time, same station?

THOMAS:

Let's see what the shrink says.

JUDY:

That could take a while. And we were scheduled for Easter Sunday.

THOMAS:

You wouldn't want to marry a mental case, would you?

JUDY:

[*Stops dancing*] This mental case, yes.

THOMAS:

It wouldn't be fair to you.

JUDY:

Honestly Tom, do you think any shrink would believe that story?

THOMAS:

No, unless he needs his own shrink, which most of them do.

JUDY:

Why are you going to one then?

THOMAS:

For Christ's sake, Judy, you just insisted that I do; you even gave me an ultimatum.

JUDY:

I didn't give you an ultimatum. I merely said that if you refuse professional help, it means that you don't care for me enough to at least …

THOMAS:

What? Have my head shrunk.

JUDY:

Oh, how I hate that kind of condescending remark. They always come from people who have so many problems that they don't dare to face them in analysis.

THOMAS:

What problems do *I* have?

JUDY:

Are you kidding? You see little black men who think they're God walking on the lake in Prospect Park…

THOMAS:

One man and not little.

JUDY:

… and you're impotent.

THOMAS:

What! You too? Et tu, Brutus? Ha ha.

JUDY:

Well, you said so yourself. And don't call me brutal; I'm just trying to help. They say cold showers help.

THOMAS:

I didn't say so. I said my ex said so.

JUDY:

Well, she should know. Oh, who cares who said so; it's the fact that matters.

THOMAS:

Judy, did you sleep with me last night?

JUDY:

You know I did.

THOMAS:

Was I impotent?

JUDY:

[*Purring*] No, darling. [*To the audience*] Not exactly.

THOMAS:

Then what the fuck are you talking about?

JUDY:

That was last night. Who knows about tonight?

THOMAS:

Judy, I think you're getting it.

JUDY:

What?

THOMAS:

Female impotence.

[BLACKOUT]

ACT TWO

SCENE ONE

THE SHRINK

Setting: DR EISBEIN and THOMAS enter carrying a chair and a couch respectively. They are placed in the classic analyst-patient position. Dr EISBEIN is soft-spoken and reasonable. He wears sneakers and jeans and an open shirt. A large medallion, which he often fingers, hangs around his neck. He has a tic in his cheek and continually crosses and uncrosses his legs.

DR EISBEIN:

[*Examining papers*] Your tests show nothing abnormal, Mr. Paulson. Frankly, I didn't expect anything else. If it weren't for your own request, I probably wouldn't have had you take them...

THOMAS:

Judy's request you mean.

DR EISBEIN:

[*Ignoring him*] Now, concerning the problem at hand: as I see it, there are several possible explanations. One, it was a hallucination. Now don't get excited. [*But Thomas is calmly resting with his eyes closed*] I just want to mention the possibilities. Two, you really saw this person in the park, and everything happened as you described it – except the walk on the water of course, which could have been some kind of optical illusion made possible by hypnotism, suggestion or the like. Three, the whole thing is a deliberate or unconscious fabrication on your part for whatever motives, conscious or unconscious, you may have. [*Thomas opens his eyes*] Before examining these possibilities ...

THOMAS:

What about a fourth possibility, Dr Eisbein?

DR EISBEIN:

Yes?

THOMAS:

That it all happened exactly as I described it, including the walk on the lake.

DR EISBEIN:

[*Long pause*] All right, we'll include it for now as a possibility. [*Writes*] Now, before examining these possibilities, I'd like to ask you a few questions – OK?

THOMAS:

Sure.

DR EISBEIN:

Have you dreamed of this person, before or after meeting him?

THOMAS:

You mean HeyZeus?

DR EISBEIN:

Yes.

THOMAS:

No.

DR EISBEIN:

Are you quite sure?

THOMAS:

Well, no, but I don't recall dreaming about him. By the way ... no, never mind.

DR EISBEIN:

Yes, what is it?

THOMAS:

I was going to say that in Spanish you dream *with* someone, not *about* them. You say I dreamed *with* you last night.

DR EISBEIN:

Is that so? What does it mean to you?

THOMAS:

Nothing. I only think the differences in languages are interesting.

DR EISBEIN:

Was Zeus Hispanic?

THOMAS:

*Hey*Zeus!

DR EISBEIN:

*Hey*Zeus then.

THOMAS:

I don't know. He didn't have an accent.

DR EISBEIN:

What about your dream life in general. Do you dream frequently?

THOMAS:

Average, I suppose.

DR EISBEIN:

What do you call average – once a week, every night?

THOMAS:

I think I dream all the time. The problem is in remembering the dreams, isn't it?

DR EISBEIN:

Do you recall a recent dream?

THOMAS:

Yes, last night. You know, names are interesting, too. Your name, Eisbein, for example, means pigs knuckles in German.

DR EISBEIN:

[*Icily*] Ice-leg.

THOMAS:

Yeah, but there's no such thing as ice-leg, whereas Eisbein is a cut of meat – a delicacy! [*Laughs*] It's cooked in the oven and served with a disgusting sauce and sauerkraut.

DR EISBEIN:

My grandfather was French, and my name is pronounced *Ace-bane*.

THOMAS:

Wow, that's cool. But that doesn't change the fact that it's a German word meaning pigs knuckles and pronounced *Ice-bine*.

DR EISBEIN:

[*Angrily*] So what … exactly … did you dream last night?

THOMAS:

Oh yeah, sorry. I was visiting Judy in another country.

DR EISBEIN:

And Judy is?

THOMAS:

My fiancée.

DR EISBEIN:

[*Writing*] What country?

THOMAS:

I don't know, I think it was Italy.

DR EISBEIN:

Go on.

THOMAS:

She had gray at her temples. I was older too. She was happy, talking animatedly. Her hands were prominent and mobile. I asked her something, I don't know what, and she said, "We're playing tonight." All the theaters here play on Sunday nights. [*Pause*] That's all.

DR EISBEIN:

What do you think about it?

THOMAS:

Judy once played Winnie in Samuel Beckett's *Happy Days*. She was supposed to be fifty years old. She was stuck up to her waist in a sandy mound but retained her good humor.

DR EISBEIN:

What's the first thing that enters your mind now?

THOMAS:

Pig's knuckles.

DR EISBEIN:

Are we going to be serious about this or not. Remember you're paying for my time.

THOMAS:

Sorry, but it really was my association. You see, after the premiere Judy and I went to a German restaurant – this was an English-speaking theater in Germany, by the way – and we ordered Eisbein. I thought it was something with ice cream, but it turned out to be, well, what it is: pig knuckles. I became a vegetarian on the spot. You remember the Good Humor ice cream man, don't you?

DR EISBEIN:

Yes, and?

THOMAS:

More association: Fear no more the heat of the Sunday.

DR EISBEIN:

I beg your pardon.

THOMAS:

Fear no more the heat o' the sun,
Nor the furious winter's rages.
Thou thy worldly task hast done,
Home art gone, and ta'en thy wages.
Golden lads and girls all must,
As chimneysweepers, come to dust.

DR EISBEIN:

The Bible?

THOMAS:

Shakespeare. Winnie says the first line – Fear no more

the heat o' the sun – out of nowhere and tries to get her husband, Willie, who's sitting behind the mound half-asleep, to repeat it. He tries, but can't get beyond "Fear no more..." It's all very enigmatic. At a party after the premiere I asked the director if he knew where it's from, and he didn't. It sounded vaguely familiar to me, so the next time I opened my Complete Works of Shakespeare to the right place by coincidence, if you believe in coincidences, I realized it's from *Cymbeline,* which I have never seen performed and didn't remember having read. It's a song recited on the death of Cloten.

DR EISBEIN:

Why do you bring it up now?

THOMAS:

Because I played Willie.

DR EISBEIN:

I see ... mmm ... Do you see a connection between this and the appearance of Jesus?

THOMAS:

HeyZeus. No [*Pause*] except, possibly ... but no, never mind.

DR EISBEIN:

No, please go on.

THOMAS:

It was a hot day, a lot of *heat of the sun* and I was feeling kind of anxious, maybe about death. After all,

I was on my way to a wake. And a storm arose, like a winter rage.

DR EISBEIN:

[*After a long pause*] You said you felt a strong attraction to this Jes ... HeyZeus. A feeling of love.

THOMAS:

That's right. It was a kind of tingling sensation.

DR EISBEIN:

Have you ever had homosexual experiences?

THOMAS:

Twice, when I was a boy. Statistically I believe that's about normal.

DR EISBEIN:

Of course. Would you mind telling me about them?

THOMAS:

Yes, I would mind.

DR EISBEIN:

Oh? Why?

THOMAS:

Because I see no point in wasting time by going in that direction.

DR EISBEIN:

[*Writing furiously*] Tell me, do you have brothers or sisters?

THOMAS:

I had a brother who died as a child.

DR EISBEIN:

How old?

THOMAS:

Nine, I was seven.

DR EISBEIN:

Do you feel any association between him and the man you met in the park?

THOMAS:

No. How about getting to your possibilities.

DR EISBEIN:

Very well. [*Flips back the pages of his note*s] The first possibility was a hallucination – or a dream.

THOMAS:

Two different things.

DR EISBEIN:

Quite. A hallucination of this magnitude would indicate mental illness. How about a dream?

THOMAS:

I was wide awake, unless you mean a vision.

DR EISBEIN:

What do you mean by that?

THOMAS:

No, I don't mean that either. It couldn't have been a vision because he kissed me. [*Touches his cheek*] I felt it but ... it wasn't as though real lips, of flesh and blood I mean, had kissed me – which wouldn't have caused this persistent tingling either. No, it wasn't a dream or a vision. Yet it might not have been a normal human body either.

DR EISBEIN:

Then you admit that he wasn't real?

THOMAS:

Yes ... I mean no. He *was* real. It's hard to explain.

DR EISBEIN:

Try.

THOMAS:

Did you ever feel someone's presence even though they weren't there?

DR EISBEIN:

No, I can't say that I have. Either they're there or they aren't. Of course, during masturbation an other's presence can be felt very vividly, but that's due to one's own ability to fantasize.

THOMAS:

That's not exactly what I have in mind. Shall I continue anyway?

DR EISBEIN:

By all means.

THOMAS:

It was like he was a felt presence who was really there, but not completely. As though he had gone and left something behind.

DR EISBEIN:

As though he'd left what behind?

THOMAS:

I don't know, like a phantom body. You've heard about people who've had a limb amputated, a leg, for example.

DR EISBEIN:

Yes, yes, go on.

THOMAS:

Yet they can still feel the leg. As if the leg is still there but emptied of its physical content.

DR EISBEIN:

Yes. [*Writes furiously*]

THOMAS:

He was like the amputated leg, the part that still lives and the amputee feels. But – and this is the tricky part – it's visible and touchable without containing its physical substance. Do you follow me? Like an ice-leg.

DR EISBEIN:

Yes, no doubt about it.

THOMAS:

No doubt about what?

DR EISBEIN:

Castration complex

THOMAS:

[*Astonished*] Are you serious?

DR EISBEIN:

Quite. But don't be put off by the word complex, which is a poor translation of the German *Gefühl*. In your case it's more of a castration *feeling*. Tell me, why do you think he kissed you?

THOMAS:

How should I know that?

DR EISBEIN:

I asked you what you *think*.

THOMAS:

All right. Perhaps for two reasons. First, because he knew what I was thinking, that I wanted to touch him just to make sure. You know, like Doubting Thomas.

DR EISBEIN:

So you weren't completely sure?

THOMAS:

Dr Eisbein, have you been listening to me at all?

DR EISBEIN:

[*Long pause*] What's the second reason?

THOMAS:

Because he loves me ... should be the first reason.

DR EISBEIN:

Now we're getting somewhere Thomas, if you don't mind my calling you that. You said that you had two homosexual experiences as a child, but you don't want to talk about them. Your lack of willingness to be open about them is a hindrance of course, but on the other hand it could be meaningful. I'll accept that for now, but I'd like you to tell me – frankly – if you ever felt sexual desire towards men. I mean ever!

THOMAS:

Oh God in heaven!

DR EISBEIN:

Apparently it's too early to confront you with that kind of reality, so let's pass on to the second possibility. What was it? [*Looks through notes*] Oh yes, that it happened as you describe it, that you really did see such a man who you imagined to have walked on the surface of the lake in Prospect Park. [*Pause*] Tell me about your mother.

THOMAS:

She's a lot of fun.

DR EISBEIN:

Domineering?

THOMAS:

Of course. Aren't they all?

DR EINSBEIN:

Oh, I wouldn't say that.

THOMAS:

[*Turns to look at him*] Wasn't your mother domineering?

DR EISBEIN:

We're talking about your mother, not mine. How was your relationship with her?

THOMAS:

Sexy as hell. And the lake reminds me of her cunt. Shall we pass on to the third possibility?

DR EISBEIN:

[*Checks his watch, then reads*] A deliberate or unconscious fabrication.

THOMAS:

Hmm. Judy thinks I'm trying to get out of marrying her by using HeyZeus as an excuse. Hey, you must know Judy, she recommended you.

DR EISBEIN:

No, Mrs Muelletonne called me about you.

THOMAS:

What is your relationship with her?

DR EISBEIN:

Doctor-patient. Why do you ask?

THOMAS:

Curiosity. Look Dr Eisbein, I do want to avoid marrying Judy. But before I met HeyZeus I *wanted* to marry her. Assuming that I'm not gay, which I'm not, there's no apparent cause for that effect.

DR EISBEIN:

What effect?

THOMAS:

Wanting to not marry Judy. I mean the effect can't come before the cause.

DR EISBEIN:

Where the unconscious is concerned, all is possible.

THOMAS:

Explain, please.

DR EISBEIN:

The real cause may have been – note that I say *may* have been – that you want to avoid marrying Judy because she reminds you of your mother. And you're attracted to her sexually for the same reason. However, since all this takes place in the unconscious, you don't recognize it as the cause, so you assign the cause to HeyZeus. The dream with Judy buried up to her neck for example…

THOMAS:

That wasn't a dream, it was a play. And she was buried up to her waist in a mound.

DR EISBEIN:

She was buried up to her waist in a play?

THOMAS:

Yes, I told you that. In the dream there was no mound.

DR EISBEIN:

Yes. In any case, the mound is significant.

THOMAS:

For Beckett maybe, but not for me.

DR EISBEIN:

The mound has a hole in it, where Judy is, er, inserted, I presume.

THOMAS:

I see what you're driving at: the mound is my mother's womb and Judy is my mother. But what's my mother doing in her own womb?

DR EISBEIN:

Where the unconscious is concerned …

THOMAS:

… all is possible. Yeah, right.

DR EISBEIN:

One shouldn't oversimplify; we must analyze this dream carefully.

THOMAS:

[*Sits up*] Hey Doc, I think you've got something. Winnie is buried up to her waist only in the first act.

You really should see some Beckett, Dr Eisbein. What's your first name, anyway?

DR EISBEIN:

[*Pleased, smiles*] Archie.

THOMAS:

Archie Eisbein! By God, that's an interesting name! You've hit the nail on the head, Archie. Winnie is being sucked down. In the second act, she's up to her shoulders in the sandy mound. She's dying. She's being sucked back into the womb of the earth. And Willie? He's got a few years to go yet. Okay, that takes care of that possibility. Let's move on to the fourth; the only one I suggested.

DR EISBEIN:

Which one was that?

THOMAS:

Look it up.

DR EISBEIN:

Oh yes, of course.

[*As EISBEIN rummages through his notes looking for the fourth possibility, THOMAS tiptoes behind him and ... off. The lights dim to out as EISBEIN notices that THOMAS has gone and looks around stupidly.*]

[BLACKOUT]

SCENE TWO

TRUE ADVERTISING

Setting: A meeting of True Advertising chaired by the Chairman of the Board: C.B., with several employees: THOMAS, MARGO and JOHN.

C.B.:

Good morning. [*Sits*]

ALL:

Good morning, C.B. [*All sit*]

C.B.:

Ms Ackhorn is sick today, so someone else will have to take the minutes.

JOHN:

She's always sick on Mondays.

MARGO:

English secretaries are always sick on Mondays. It has something to do with their National Health Plan. She once told me that the people in Northern Ireland don't want to separate from Britain because they'd lose their health insurance.

JOHN:

Maybe we should revert to colonial status. I wouldn't mind working four days a week and have free health insurance.

C.B.:

That has nothing to do with it; she's sick, that's all.

MARGO:

Force of habit.

C.B.:

One must overlook some things in order to have a good English secretary. Who would like to keep the minutes?

MARGO:

What's good about her, except the accent?

JOHN:

Her legs.

C.B.:

She's got class – a most important attribute in this business, especially since it lacks so many others. But the purpose of this meeting is not to discuss Ms Ackhorn. Will you kindly keep the minutes, Margo?

MARGO:

Not a chance.

JOHN:

I'll do it, C.B.

C.B.:

Thank you, John. Please read the previous meeting's minutes. [*Holds out a sheet of paper. John goes to him, takes it and returns to his place*]

JOHN:

[*Reads in a monotone*] The Chairman opened the meeting at 9:30 a.m. In Ms Ackhorn's absence, John Savage read the minutes of the previous meeting and agreed to keep the minutes of this meeting. The previous meeting's minutes were approved unanimously. John Savage reported on the applicants for the artist opening. The Board considered several resumes and drawings and decided to accept the Chairman's recommendation and hire Ms Bubbles Bardot ...

C.B.:

Bubba Bardot ... her name is Bubba Bardot. She's French, very creative.

JOHN:

[Correcting his report] Bubba Bardot. Margo Thornton reported meeting with the V.P. of the Now Corporation at a cocktail party in Washington and about his interest in our agency. It was agreed that she would follow up this lead. Thomas Paulson described an idea he proposed to use in connection with the American Style Travel Agency account. It was judged by the Board to be highly original, but somewhat daring. Mr Paulson was asked to develop it further. The Chairman gave a projection of the year's financial results, which are positive, but in need of improvement. The meeting was adjourned at 10:35 a.m. [*Pause*] I move that the minutes be approved.

MARGO:

Seconded.

C.B.:

Thomas?

THOMAS:

Yeah, sure.

C.B.:

Minutes approved unanimously. Now to the second item on the agenda. This is a humdinger. I asked Margo not to let it out of the bag until this meeting. Go ahead Margo, please.

MARGO:

As I mentioned at the previous meeting, I met Dr. Kellog, the V.P. of the Now Corporation, at a cocktail party in Washington. He's a charming man, for someone so powerful, and had even heard about us. He was especially impressed by the travel agency ads.

C.B.:

That's you, Thomas. Excuse me, Margo.

MARGO:

Right, but if I may say so, I had the impression that he liked me as well.

C.B.:

[*Loud laugh*] I have no doubt of that, my dear.

MARGO:

He asked for my telephone number for the next time he'd be in New York. He's from Texas of course.

JOHN:

Home or office?

MARGO:

Both.

JOHN:

And you gave them to him?

MARGO:

Of course, why not?

JOHN:

Why yes, if it was only business?

MARGO:

It wasn't, darling.

C.B. [*Loud laugh*] What a gal! Best damn salesman in the business.

JOHN:

That depends on what she's selling.

MARGO:

What exactly do you mean by that?

JOHN:

You know what I mean.

MARGO:

Unfortunately, I do. Anyway, he called me last week.

JOHN:

At the office?

MARGO:

That may have been your business once, but it no

longer is, so please stop interrupting. He asked me to dinner and, to make a long story short, we've got a sizable chunk of Now's advertising budget.

JOHN:

Just like that?

MARGO:

No, not just like that. I said I was making a long story short – or do you want all the lurid details to put in the minutes?

C.B.:

Dr. Kellog telephoned me the next morning to confirm their desire that we take over a certain line of advertising for them. The contract will be signed on Friday. It's a million-dollar account, the biggest in True Advertising's history. Cheer up, John. You take some things too seriously. Margo got this business based on our own track record – as well as her powers of persuasion.

MARGO:

God, we've been divorced for over a year. I don't see why you have anything to say about with whom I have dinner ... or even sleep with if I want.

JOHN:

I was only teasing you. [*Dejected*] Congratulations.

MARGO:

Thanks.

THOMAS:

Which of their lines are we supposed to sell? They make everything from toilet paper to atomic bombs.

C.B.:

I didn't know they're into toilet paper, and if they make atomic bombs, they won't be advertising it.

THOMAS:

Why not? We could call it "the solution to the population explosion".

MARGO:

Very funny. But the emphasis will be on Now's image in respect to its activities in the energy field.

THOMAS:

Atomic energy?

MARGO:

We prefer to call it nuclear energy. That's the kind of energy they produce.

THOMAS:

Which presents certain problems.

MARGO:

Which ones do you have in mind?

THOMAS:

Well, let's see. Radioactive waste from the atomic energy plants that have a half-life of a few thousand years or so, and that includes the plants themselves that become deadly structures of radioactivity after about thirty years – and there's no place to put it all. Then there's the security issue and the fact that the things aren't even economically viable. I think any reasonably intelligent person – and I presume that we are all reasonably intelligent here – must realize that atomic energy is one of the biggest rip-offs in history.

MARGO:

Your Socratic argument implies that anyone who disagrees with you isn't reasonably intelligent. At least you'll concede that there have been so many rip-offs in history that it's a little presumptuous to categorically state that this is one of the biggest – assuming that it is one at all.

THOMAS:

Can you think of a bigger one?

MARGO:

How about the immaculate conception?

THOMAS:

[*Raises his thumb in acknowledgment*]

C.B.:

Do you realize what an interesting challenge it is for us? To emphasize the positive aspects and make the public forget the negative ones. It's nuclear energy, by the way.

THOMAS:

What positive aspects?

JOHN:

[*After a long pause*] It's cleaner than coal.

THOMAS:

That's true.

C.B.:

Yes, of course. And Dr. Kellog will advise us on that; there must be more.

THOMAS:

I don't like it.

C.B.:

That has nothing to do with it, Tom. It's your ideas that count, not what you like or don't like.

THOMAS:

Yeah, I guess so. I have an idea for an ad.

C.B.:

Fine, let's hear it.

THOMAS:

A huge mushroom cloud, caption: Progress – NOW.

C.B.:

Very funny. You have a great sense of humor. Now just channel it in the right direction.

THOMAS:

O.K., how about this? It's the future. Children are playing in an ultra-modern nursery school. Wholesome teachers in white smocks smiling –

MARGO:

Racially mixed.

THOMAS:

Of course. Caption: Make their future possible – NOW!

C.B.:

Tom, you're a genius, I always said so. Maybe you can get together with the new artist; what's his name again?

JOHN:

Boyd.

C.B.:

That's right. See if you can work something out with him. The approach is just right: accentuate the positive.

THOMAS:

The kids are all deformed, hunchbacks, fin-like arms, cyclops eyes, bald ...

JOHN:

That's not the direction C.B. has in mind, Paulson.

THOMAS:

I know that, but why shouldn't we begin thinking about what we're doing? The other day I was in Prospect Park ...

MARGO:

In Brooklyn?

THOMAS:

Yes. And this guy suddenly appeared, a very unusual guy, I mean beautiful, and he walked on the lake.

C.B.:

They produce energy, and we have an energy crisis. What more do you want? And that's not all. There's a good chance that we'll get a piece of the American Outdoor Brands Corporation account.

JOHN:

Wow! That's wonderful, C.B. How'd you swing that?

C.B.:

I know the PR Director. He's also a member of the National Rifle Association. And we're both Masons.

THOMAS:

Wait a minute. Outdoor Brands. I remember now. That's Smith & Wesson, cowboys and Indians, they changed their name.

C.B.:

It's actually a new company, of which Smith & Wesson is a branch.

THOMAS:

Smith & Wesson made, and makes, the pistol that won the West. You know, John Wayne, Billy the Kid.

C.B.:

Actually, nowadays they supply most of the country's police departments.

MARGO:

Do they only make guns?

C.B.:

Oh no, they also make rifles, knives, all kinds of outdoor stuff. Hence the name.

THOMAS:

My god, from travel agencies to atomic bombs and guns.

C.B.:

I can understand how you feel, Tom. But this is the real world and we're part of it. It's not our job to judge what our clients do, but to help them achieve their goals.

THOMAS:

Whatever they may be?

C.B.:

Their goal is to make money ... yes, money, which, strictly speaking, is also ours. Is there anything wrong with that? Of course not. It's the goal of our whole society and it's a wonderfully unhypocritical goal. And we say so and we mean it. That's what makes America so great.

THOMAS:

What if it's an immoral goal?

C.B.:

It can't be immoral; it's unpatriotic to imply that it is.

Life, liberty and the pursuit of happiness, freedom of the press and their ads, that's what we've got ... especially the latter. That's what True Advertising stands for.

THOMAS:

The truth is supposed to make us free.

JOHN:

And what, may I ask, is the truth, in your humble opinion.

THOMAS:

It isn't what True Advertising does. But since you ask, I'd like to tell you about something that happened to me in the park ...

C.B.:

All this amateur philosophy is very interesting if we had time for it. But we've got contracts to close with two really important clients by next week – three working days actually, and we gotta be prepared to talk sense and dollars and cents with them. So let's get down to business ... please!

THOMAS:

I say we turn them down.

C.B.:

On what grounds?

THOMAS:

On moral grounds.

C.B.:

[*Violently*] Are you mad? It would ruin us. Everyone on the street would know about it immediately. Our reputation would be shattered. Furthermore, I beg to remind you that we have a silent partner with a 50% interest – Mrs. Jonathan Winter, a senile old lady sitting in her palatial apartment on Riverside Drive watching TV all day and probably never heard of us. But her trustees and her grandchildren sure as hell have and there'd be holy hell to pay if we ever tried to turn down such lucrative business.

THOMAS:

Parasites.

MARGO:

But a fact of life.

THOMAS:

Count me out.

MARGO:

Of what, life?

THOMAS:

No, the game.

C.B.:

[*Almost screaming*] What do you mean, count you out. You're our idea man! Who the fuck do you think you are, anyway?

THOMAS:

[*Calmly*] The idea man. I just had an idea, the greatest of my career. Count me out of True Advertising. Or fire me, I'd prefer that.

JOHN:

To be a martyr?

THOMAS:

To collect unemployment insurance. [*Stands and starts off*]

C.B.:

Oh, for the love of Christ!

[*THOMAS stops, turns and looks at C.B. for a moment, then exits*]

JOHN:

What's eating him?

MARGO:

He said something happened in the park. I wonder what.

C.B.:

What in hell do I care what happened in the park. This is an advertising agency, not a fucking zoo. Sorry Margo.

JOHN:

He'll be back.

MARGO:

No, he won't.

JOHN:

How do you know?

MARGO:

Intuition: Thomas Paulson won't be back.

[BLACKOUT]

SCENE THREE

THE BISHOP

Setting: Two chairs downstage center. BISHOP CASEY sits facing the audience. Thomas sits at a 90-degree angle to him at his left. A desk is behind them upon which is a crucifix. The BISHOP sits with his legs spread. He repeatedly lifts his hand to his ear and/or inclines his head toward THOMAS when the latter speaks. He is not hearing his confession, but falls into this posture by force of habit.

BISHOP CASEY:

How long has it been since we last saw each other, Thomas?

THOMAS:

It must be a good twenty years, Father ... I mean Bishop Casey.

BISHOP CASEY:

You were considering entering the priesthood, if I remember correctly.

THOMAS:

Not exactly. I was on the St. Francis Prep basketball team you coached.

BISHOP CASEY:

Yes, of course. I thought you were interested in the priesthood as well. A forward, weren't you?

THOMAS:

No, point guard.

BISHOP CASEY:

That's right. Well, I must admit that your story is an extraordinary one. However, you do realize that you could have gone to your parish priest.

THOMAS:

I don't have a parish priest.

BISHOP CASEY:

Oh? It's terrible the shortage of priests. We could certainly use you, Thomas. Which parish do you live in now?

THOMAS:

It's not that. I left the Church long ago; no church, no parish priest.

BISHOP CASEY:

I remember now, Tommy Paulson. You had a great jump shot.

THOMAS:

Relatively great.

BISHOP CASEY:

When did you start having doubts about the faith?

THOMAS:

A long time ago, even then, when I played basketball for St. Francis. But I didn't tell anyone, I was afraid I wouldn't be allowed to play. At least it didn't affect my jump shot.

BISHOP CASEY:

You always were fresh, weren't you. Maybe you should tell me about it now. How did it happen?

THOMAS:

What?

BISHOP CASEY:

Your loss of faith.

THOMAS:

It was the index of forbidden books. I was leaving mass one Sunday with a friend and they handed us the list at the door. *The Three Musketeers* were on it. I had just finished reading it and I had every intention of reading the sequel as soon as I could get my hands on it, which would have been a sin for a Catholic, so I decided to stop being one. Of course it wasn't that easy. But that was the beginning of the process. Do you know why *The Three Musketeers* is on it, Bishop Casey?

BISHOP CASEY:

As a matter of fact, no.

THOMAS:

Well then, I'll tell you. One of the main characters, Cardinal Richelieu, is a really bad guy, which of course is impossible. I mean how can a Cardinal be bad? So, ban the book.

BISHOP CASEY:

It seems a trivial reason to leave the Church.

THOMAS:

Not to me.

BISHOP CASEY:

You should have sought guidance.

THOMAS:

What for? It was right there in black and white. My favorite book forbidden to me.

BISHOP CASEY:

Why have you come to me now then?

THOMAS:

I liked you when you were the coach and I thought now that you are a bishop you must know about these things. I'd be interested in knowing, for example, if anyone else has seen him.

BISHOP CASEY:

Who?

THOMAS:

HeyZeus.

BISHOP CASEY:

Oh, well, every now and again someone thinks they have, although it's usually the virgin. [*Thinks*] There's a woman in Germany right now who has the stigmata.

THOMAS:

Stigmata?

BISHOP CASEY:

The wounds of Christ: five of them, on her hands, feet and breast.

THOMAS:

Oh yeah, of course. I mean no, I haven't heard about her. I wonder why.

BISHOP CASEY:

Because it's hardly news, except in Germany, and there only for a while.

THOMAS:

Why is that? Sounds like big news to me.

BISHOP CASEY:

It's only news about the power of suggestion. She also claims to experience Jesus – in the flesh.

THOMAS:

Wow! Second coming?

BISHOP CASEY:

Not exactly. Time travel.

THOMAS:

Oh. I assume she's a German peasant girl, like the others.

BISHOP CASEY:

Actually she's an architect. And she's not even Catholic

THOMAS:

Protestant?

BISHOP CASEY:

Jewish.

THOMAS:

Oh my God, that's so cool!

BISHOP CASEY:

It's ludicrous.

THOMAS:

But has anyone really seen him, according to the Church?

BISHOP CASEY:

Not that I know of. That's why I can't help wondering why you should?

THOMAS:

I've asked myself the same question.

BISHOP CASEY:

And why he should be black.

THOMAS:

Why not? There are black Madonnas in Poland, Brazil and Catalonia, even in Switzerland.

BISHOP CASEY:

Switzerland?

THOMAS:

Sure. There's a town in Switzerland, Einsiedeln, that has a cathedral with a black Madonna in it – a statue of course – and she's holding a black Jesus in her arms. I don't know why they're black, do you?

BISHOP CASEY:

No, but …

THOMAS:

In Brazil it's because someone found a small black Madonna figure in a river a half a century ago.

BISHOP CASEY:

I heard about it. They built a church for it in Rio de Janeiro.

THOMAS:

Sao Paulo. It must be one of the ugliest churches in existence.

BISHOP CASEY:

Have you seen it, personally?

THOMAS:

Yes, when I was in the peace Corp. It's on the highway that connects Sao Paulo with Rio. From the outside it looks like a huge warehouse; inside like an over-sized airplane hangar. I guess a better analogy would be a supermarket. There's even a gas station in the parking lot. The church is made of brick with one endlessly repeating design. The Madonna's the size of a large doll. It's encased in a glass vault beside the main altar. You buy a ticket at the box office. I forget how much it costs – not much – and wait in line between aluminum rails that funnel you up to the altar. People like to touch in Brazil, or anywhere I guess, but the Madonna is behind glass, for security reasons probably, so all they can touch is a metal rod that extends out through the glass from the doll's foot. It's obviously a big deal for them to see the doll and touch the rod. They kneel before it and some of them even cry. It's moving and repellent at the same time. But she's black all right.

BISHOP CASEY:

That's understandable. Brazil has many black people.

THOMAS:

Yes, one can assume a certain identification. But not in Switzerland – no racial identification possible there.

BISHOP CASEY:

Either way, Jesus was not black.

THOMAS:

No, he was a Jew.

BISHOP CASEY:

So how do you explain that the person you saw and take to be him is black.

THOMAS:

I can't explain it. But given the existence of black Madonnas, I don't think it's so strange.

BISHOP CASEY:

The whole thing is strange.

THOMAS:

You don't believe it then?

BISHOP CASEY:

You haven't said anything convincing. So why should I?

THOMAS:

Walking on the water? That doesn't happen every day.

BISHOP CASEY:

An optical illusion, your imagination, a trick, who knows? It's only your word for it; you have no witnesses, if I understood you correctly.

THOMAS:

I can understand you having doubts, but not an outright rejection without really knowing. What if I'm telling the truth and it was really him?

BISHOP CASEY:

That's hardly likely.

THOMAS:

Why? He's supposed to come back, isn't he?

BISHOP CASEY:

Wrong color, wrong manner. Your friend doesn't coincide in any way with what we know of him.

THOMAS:

What do you know of him if you haven't seen or heard him?

BISHOP CASEY:

We have the Gospels, which give an exact description.

THOMAS:

That was two thousand years ago. I mean now. Besides, I suspect there are more sides to him than what's in the gospels.

BISHOP CASEY:

Perhaps you intend to write a Fifth Gospel with the Beatles supplying the music; or another Jesus Christ Superstar.

THOMAS:

Now you're getting fresh, Bishop Casey.

BISHOP CASEY:

[*After a long pause*] There is a great contradiction in all this, which constitutes the main reason why your story is unacceptable.

THOMAS:

Aside from it being crazy?

BISHOP CASEY:

Aside from that. If Jesus were to come back, now, why would he appear to you and not to the Church? Why should he appear to someone who does not even belong to the Church? Our Lord cannot simply ignore his own Church!

THOMAS:

If it's his, he can do what he likes with it, I should think.

BISHOP CASEY:

You think wrong. For two thousand years we have been carrying out his mission. There have been a few mistakes, it's true. But we have learned from them.

THOMAS:

Whatever that means.

BISHOP CASEY:

Just be quiet a minute, will you. The Church has His and its own dignity and truth to uphold. And now you, Tom Paulson, jump-shot artist, turn up and say that he has returned, black, in blue jeans and whistling Dixie.

THOMAS:

Humming ... *Let It Be*.

BISHOP CASEY:

It would be irresponsible, unthinkable for him to do such a thing. Ergo, it's unacceptable.

THOMAS:

Maybe he has a different concept of responsibility.

BISHOP CASEY:

All the more reason to protect him from himself, to protect his name and his work. I mean if it happened to really be ... him, which of course it isn't.

THOMAS:

What you're saying, Father – Bishop Casey – is that you, and/or your Church, know more about what's needed than the one you're supposed to be representing.

BISHOP CASEY:

You're a regular doubting Thomas, aren't you. I'm only stating why it couldn't be him. I'd advise you, Thomas Paulson, to not broadcast your – er – revelation and make a fool of yourself.

THOMAS:

That's your only advice?

BISHOP CASEY:

No. Come back to the Church and heed its teachings.

THOMAS:

So, it's either the Church or him?

BISHOP CASEY:

Your him, yes. [*Looks closely at THOMAS*] What's that on your cheek? I didn't notice it before.

THOMAS:

You didn't look at me before. But anyway, what's wrong with my cheek?

BISHOP CASEY:

There's a red mark on it.

THOMAS:

[*Touches his cheek*] Here?

BISHOP CASEY:

It must be a rash.

THOMAS:

Where?

BISHOP CASEY:

[*Goes behind the desk, takes a mirror from a drawer and hands it to THOMAS*] Do you mean to tell me that you didn't have it before?

THOMAS:

[*Looking in the mirror*] Wow! It wasn't there this morning when I shaved. It's where he kissed me.

BISHOP CASEY:

This is getting grotesque, distinctly hysterical.

THOMAS:

Hysterical?

BISHOP CASEY:

In the medical sense: a physical manifestation of a psychic disturbance.

THOMAS:

Do you think stigmata are hysterical.

BISHOP CASEY:

If you are referring to that woman in Germany, I'd say yes, definitely. She and many others.

THOMAS:

Like Saint Francis?

BISHOP CASEY:

Saints recognized by the Church had genuine stigmata; the rest are hysterical. Besides, by definition, stigmata represent Christ's wounds, not his kisses. You're not a saint, are you?

THOMAS:

No, of course not. I can't explain why he picked me. Maybe I'm not the only one.

BISHOP CASEY:

[*Reverting to his confessional pose*] Go to a doctor, have it treated. Cortisone will take care of it.

THOMAS:

Do you really think so?

BISHOP CASEY:

Yes, it works wonders. I have eczema too. Cortisone treatments offer the only relief.

THOMAS:

[*Looks closely at him*] Where?

BISHOP CASEY:

Not on my face.

THOMAS:

Where?

BISHOP CASEY:

[*Scratches his crotch, smiles*] Would you like to see?

THOMAS:

Actually … no.

BISHOP CASEY:

The itching would be intolerable if it weren't for the cortisone. Are you sure you don't want to see?

THOMAS:

[*Touching his cheek*] This doesn't itch at all, it tingles. And it's not intolerable; it's most agreeable.

BISHOP CASEY:

All the more reason to have it treated.

THOMAS:

You don't like it, do you? Evidence like this disturbs you. Like Red Hook.

BISHOP CASEY:

Red Hook?

THOMAS:

A neighborhood in Brooklyn where the poverty rate is over fifty percent and most of the people live on food stamps. It also has the most births to teen mothers in the city. It's part of your diocese. Do you know where it is?

BISHOP CASEY:

Of course, I know where it is.

THOMAS:

When did you last visit it?

BISHOP CASEY:

Why should I visit Red Hook?

THOMAS:

The people are very poor there. It reminds me of the *favelas* in Brazil. And Jesus hung out with the poor, didn't he?

BISHOP CASEY:

First of all, you can't compare Brooklyn with Brazil. And secondly, the poor will be with us always, according to Jesus.

THOMAS:

The difference between the favelas in Brazil and the poverty in Red Hook is that in Brazil it's horizontal in shacks and in the Red Hook projects it's vertical.

BISHOP CASEY:

I think we have a soup kitchen there.

THOMAS:

Where exactly?

BISHOP CASEY:

Our Lady of … Something.

THOMAS:

Congratulations! You're a bishop with a soup kitchen, you think. And I'm an ad man with a big mouth, suddenly ... Hey, Bishop Casey, what do you say we get together and do an advertising campaign about Red Hook – awaken social consciousness, as they say. Your money and my know-how. This advertisement is brought to you by the archdiocese ... no, then you'd be an archbishop, and you ain't there yet. This announcement is brought to you by the diocese of Brooklyn. At the bottom there's a pic of a dead mutilated cat. Text. Who killed this cat? A ten-year-old child. Why? Because in Red Hook children's souls are destroyed. Who destroys them? We do. The admen, the bishops, the bankers, the drug dealers, the oligarchs. And let us not forget the politicians and the turnstile teachers. And the so-called social media people – assassins of the first order. No bloody Genghis Kahn or Hitler was as efficient a killer as those creative geniuses. So, what can you do? Stop! Get off the bandwagon! Something like that Bishop Casey. What do you think?

BISHOP CASEY:

You're crazy. You'd better get hold of yourself before it's too late and you explode.

THOMAS:

That's exactly what I feel like doing: exploding. Wham! Don't worry Bishop Casey, I won't do it here. It'd be wasted effort. You'd have me scraped off the walls in no time.

BISHOP CASEY:

You'll have to leave now. I have a busy appointment schedule today. [*Stands*] I wish I could say it's been a pleasure seeing you again.

THOMAS:

It hasn't?

BISHOP CASEY:

Decidedly not. Go now, and God bless you.

THOMAS:

Thanks Father, I mean Bishop. Thanks very much. [*Exits*]

[**BLACKOUT**, *except for the crucifix, which glows in the dark for a few seconds*]

ACT THREE

SCENE ONE

PROSPECT PARK REDUX

Setting: FIRST MAN enters, passes in front of THOMAS.

THOMAS:

Excuse me. Did you see a black man wearing jeans and a blue t-shirt here in the park?

FIRST MAN:

[*Stops, peers closely at THOMAS*] No, and I hope to God I don't. [*Exit*]

THOMAS:

[*To the audience*] See what I mean? The inhabitants of Brooklyn are seldom ambiguous.

[*ICE AGENT enters*]

THOMAS:

Did you see a black man wearing jeans and a blue t-shirt here in the park?

ICE AGENT:

Sure, plenty of them. So what?

THOMAS:

[*Stands*] You did? Where?

ICE AGENT:

Are you kidding me? This park is full of black guys in t-shirts.

THOMAS:

This one is in his twenties, probably. About my height. His name is HeyZeus.

ICE AGENT:

What do you want with him?

THOMAS:

I only want to talk to him.

ICE AGENT:

I want to know why you want to talk to him. Are you a cop? If you are, show me your badge.

THOMAS:

No, I'm not.

ICE AGENT:

A private eye?

THOMAS:

No, look, just forget it, will you.

ICE AGENT:

Are you out to get him? Did he rape your wife?

THOMAS:

[*Sits, puts his head in his hands*] No.

ICE AGENT:

Your girlfriend then? Your sister?

THOMAS:

Fuck off!

ICE AGENT:

Are you looking for a black guy or not? If not, why'd you ask? Wait, I know. You're looking for a fix. First you ask me if I saw a black guy in jeans and a blue t-shirt in the park and then you tell me to get lost. What if I did see him? Do you want to know where? Over by the boathouse. A black guy in jeans and a blue t-shirt. Do you know him?

THOMAS:

Who are you anyway?

ICE AGENT:

[Flips open his wallet, shows his ID to Thomas.] Immigration and Customs Enforcement, also known as ICE.

THOMAS:

But HeyZeus is American ... from Brooklyn.

ICE AGENT:

We'll see about that. It's about time this park was cleaned up and the junkies put where they belong. [*Exit*]

[*A young woman enters, approaches THOMAS and sits next to him on the bench, tilts her head and smiles at the audience*]

MAGDALENA:

Hello.

THOMAS:

[*Startled, looks up*] Hello.

MAGDALENA:

I'm Magdalena. I overheard your conversation with that man. It's awful that some people are so nasty and suspicious. I was standing over there waiting for someone too. But he didn't come, so I guess I'm stood up. That's not so bad though. Probably it means something when you're stood up. [*Pause*] It's nice here in front of the lake at this time of day, but a bit chilly. I don't mind the cold if I'm dressed warmly. Do you? I had to screw up my courage to come over and sit like this next to a stranger, but I know there's no danger. I could see that you're nice and that you have something serious on your mind, and that's why you asked those men if they'd seen your friend. He is your friend, isn't he?

THOMAS:

Not really.

MAGDALENA:

If you don't mind my asking – if you do, just ignore

the question, ignore me if you like, but if you don't mind my asking, who's the guy you're waiting for?

THOMAS:

Did you see him, Magdalena?

MAGDALENA:

I don't know. Can you tell me more about him?

THOMAS:

He can walk on water.

MAGDALENA:

Wow! That's a good trick I must say. Where have I heard that before? It sounds familiar.

THOMAS:

You don't know?

MAGDALENA:

Mary Poppins? No, she flew.

THOMAS:

[*Shakes his head*] Amazing!

MAGDALENA:

It certainly is if someone can walk on water. I mean Mary Poppins isn't real. Hey, is this a riddle? If you mean in winter, when the lake is frozen over. Is that the answer?

THOMAS:

No, it was in the spring.

MAGDALENA:

That makes it harder. Let me think. [*Thinks*] Oh, I'm no good at riddles.

THOMAS:

It's not a riddle.

MAGDALENA:

It's not? Then you're really waiting for someone who can really walk on water?

THOMAS:

That's right.

MAGDALENA:

How do you know he can do it?

THOMAS:

I saw him, right here on the lake. [*Stands, walks to the edge of the stage*] He came from the lake, then walked out onto the lake, about fifteen yards, then turned around and walked back.

MAGDALENA [*Stands*]:

That's really something. Why do you think he did it?

THOMAS:

I don't know.

MAGDALENA:

Didn't he say?

THOMAS:

No.

MAGDALENA:

Was there a storm?

THOMAS:

How did you know that?

MAGDALENA:

Isn't that funny? There's this famous person – Didn't he walk on the water during a storm, too? What's your friend's name? You told that man, but I didn't get it.

THOMAS:

HeyZeus.

MAGDALENA:

Sounds Greek.

THOMAS:

Sounds more like Spanish for Jesus,

MAGDALENA:

Oh sure! It was Jesus who walked on the water, but that was a long time ago.

THOMAS:

He's supposed to come back ... I think

MAGDALENA:

Now?

THOMAS:

Well, actually I don't know when.

MAGDALENA:

Anyway, it must have been him. I mean nobody else

can walk on water, right?

THOMAS:

I'm not so sure anymore; nobody believes me.

MAGDALENA:

Who knows about him?

THOMAS:

I've told – or tried to tell – some friends, my girlfriend, a psychiatrist, a bishop, my boss, and a theater audience. [*Looks at audience*]

MAGDALENA:

Maybe they aren't the right people to tell. *I* believe you.

THOMAS:

I think you do. I think you really do. Why?

MAGDALENA:

Why not?

THOMAS:

It's not convincing.

MAGDALENA:

It's not?

THOMAS:

Of course not. First of all, HeyZeus is black and Jesus wasn't. And why should he appear to me, of all people, without witnesses. He must have known nobody would believe me.

MAGDALENA:

If he's black it must be because he was born into a black family.

THOMAS:

[*Sighs*] Obviously.

MAGDALENA:

That last time he was born into a white Jewish family. So what's the big deal?

THOMAS:

It's a big deal because, well, just because.

MAGDALENA:

And that he appeared to you doesn't seem so strange to me. You're nice.

THOMAS:

Oh great, that's a good reason.

MAGDALENA:

Sure it is. Of course there may be other reasons as well.

THOMAS:

Well, it's not good enough for me.

MAGDALENA:

It makes it a little harder for you that there were no witnesses, but that doesn't prove anything as far as whether he's real or not.

THOMAS:

May I ask you a question?

MAGDALENA:

Sure, go ahead.

THOMAS:

Why are you dressed that way? And your hair ...

MAGDALENA:

Everyone who doesn't know asks me that sooner or later. I thought you might know without asking.

THOMAS:

Sorry, but I don't know.

MAGDALENA:

Neither do I. That's the problem, if there is one.

THOMAS:

If you don't know yourself, how can you expect me to know?

MAGDALENA:

You look like you might know. Someone must know. Maybe HeyZeus does.

THOMAS:

They're your clothes and your hair. You must have a reason for making yourself up that way.

MAGDALENA:

But I really don't. Lots of people have asked me, including my parents, but I can never answer them.

THOMAS:

Let's analyze it.

MAGDALENA:

[*Happily*] Okay!

THOMAS:

Do you think your hair looks good that way?

MAGDALENA:

No, it looks awful.

THOMAS:

What do your parents say about it?

MAGDALENA:

They say it looks awful. Everyone says it looks awful. I think it's nice though.

THOMAS:

Do you realize it's absurd to think that something that looks awful is nice?

MAGDALENA:

Yes, but it's nice anyway.

THOMAS:

Do you have a boyfriend?

MAGDALENA:

Yes, at least I think so, but he stood me up.

THOMAS:

What does he say about your hair?

MAGDALENA:

He thinks it looks awful too, but he likes it. *His* looks even awfuller.

THOMAS:

And he thinks it's nice, I guess.

MAGDALENA:

No, but he doesn't want to be nice. He says nice is how they want us to look so he doesn't want to look that way.

THOMAS:

Who's they?

MAGDALENA:

Everybody. His parents, his boss, you, everybody.

THOMAS:

So, he does it out of spite.

MAGDALENA:

I don't know why he does it, but that's what he says.

THOMAS:

Maybe you both do it to spite people who have other norms.

MAGDALENA:

Oh no! I wouldn't want to spite anybody. I just think it's nice.

THOMAS:

Don't you care what other people think?

MAGDALENA:

No.

THOMAS:

Not at all?

MAGDALENA:

Not what they think about me. I care about what they think about other people. What that man said about you isn't nice at all. Do you care what he thinks about you?

THOMAS:

I don't know.

MAGDALENA:

I do. It hurt me to hear him talk to you that way. But if he talked to me that way, I wouldn't care at all. People think they can tell what you're like by your hair or your clothes or your nose or your color – but they can't. They can't tell what you're like at all without getting to know you, and even then, it's awful hard.

THOMAS:

If you paint your hair orange and blue and wear crazy clothes it doesn't make it easier.

MAGDALENA:

I suppose not. Do you know how I know that you're nice?

THOMAS:

Haven't a clue. In fact, you may be mistaken. It depends on what you mean by nice.

MAGDALENA:

Oh no, I'm never mistaken about such things, at least I haven't been, yet. I know because I can see that you are nice.

THOMAS:

I thought you just said you can't tell by outer appearances.

MAGDALENA:

Did you ever hear of an aura?

THOMAS:

Oh god, please don't tell me that you can see my aura.

MAGDALENA:

Why not?

THOMAS:

Because I don't believe in such things.

MAGDALENA:

You believe that HeyZeus walked on the lake. So why don't you believe I can see auras?

THOMAS:

Touché. But anyway, I can't really say that I believe he walked on the lake. I can only definitively say that he appeared to me to be walking on the lake.

MAGDALENA:

That's the same thing. You probably saw his aura – or phantom – walking on the lake. If his regular body – if he has one – tried to walk on the lake he'd sink. Everyone knows that.

THOMAS:

I don't see auras, never saw one in my life.

MAGDALENA:

He made you see it. It's very hard to make others see your aura if they can't see it naturally. Only the gods can do that.

THOMAS:

You're a very strange girl. Do you know that? [*She smiles*] What does your aura look like?

MAGDALENA:

I don't know. I can't see my own aura; only other people's.

THOMAS:

So, according to you, HeyZeus made me see his aura, which means he's God.

MAGDALENA:

I didn't say he's God, only *a* god, the son of God ... sort of.

THOMAS:

How do you know that?

MAGDALENA:

HeyZeus told me.

THOMAS:

So, you know him?

MAGDALENA:

Yes. I didn't want to tell you right away because we have to be careful. But if Hey made you see his aura you must be okay.

THOMAS:

You call him Hey? [*Laughs*] And who's we? And why do you have to be careful?

MAGDALENA:

We are Hey's friends. And we have to be careful because they're looking for him. So, he usually hangs out in the African-American or Latino neighborhoods. Sometimes he comes here to Prospect Park for meetings. In the boathouse. [*Points*]

THOMAS:

Who's they, that are looking for him?

MAGDALENA:

Cops mostly.

THOMAS:

Why are the cops looking for him?

MAGDALENA:

The Church complained about him.

THOMAS:

The Church? But why?

MAGDALENA:

They say he's a drug dealer, but that's not true. They don't like him because they don't want someone like him butting in on their territory.

THOMAS:

Their territory? What do you mean? Brooklyn?

MAGDALENA:

No, silly, people's souls. The CIA doesn't like him either, because he's working for peace.

THOMAS:

Wait a minute now. If HeyZeus is Jesus come back – the long awaited second coming – why should the Church not like him? They should love him.

MAGDALENA:

Yeah, go figure.

[ICE AGENT enters accompanied by a policeman]

ICE AGENT:

There he is, Officer Pilato, better draw your gun.

OFFICER PILATO:

I'll decide when to draw. Who's the girl?

ICE AGENT:

Maybe she's a decoy.

OFFICER PILATO:

For what?

ICE AGENT:

How should I know. These people are tricky.

OFFICER PILATO:

[*Approaches THOMAS*] Can I see your ID, sir?

THOMAS:

Who me? Why?

OFFICER PILATO:

Never mind why, just let's see your ID.

THOMAS:

I only have a driver's license.

OFFICER PILATO:

Okay, let's see it.

THOMAS:

[*Shows license*] I'd like to know what this is all about.

OFFICER PILATO:

Turn around and spread your arms.

THOMAS:

What the devil! [*Cop turns him around and searches him*]

OFFICER PILATO:

What are you doing here?

THOMAS:

Nothing. Any law against that?

ICE AGENT:

He's waiting for a fix from some black guy. I heard him. Or he's selling the stuff. There's a law against that.

OFFICER PILATO:

[*Puts on his eyeglasses and reads from a paper*] This area of the park is a notorious contact point for drug dealers. We have orders to follow up all leads. [*Puts paper back in his pocket*] Now, who's this black friend you're waiting for?

THOMAS:

The person you mean is not my friend, I barely know him. Anyway, I was actually waiting for her – and she arrived. [*to MAGDALENA*] Isn't that right?

MAGDALENA:

[*After a rather long pause*] Yes. [*Duck quacks*]

ICE AGENT:

He told me he's waiting for a black man – Hey Zoos, or something.

OFFICER PILATO:

Hispanic?

ICE AGENT:
Likely.

OFFICER PILATO:
[*To THOMAS*] What about it sir, are you waitin' for a spic called Hey Zoos or something?

THOMAS:
No, I'm not. [*Duck quacks*]

OFFICER PILATO:
What's that?

MAGDALENA:
A duck.

ICE AGENT:
It may be a signal. They use bird calls and all kinds of stuff. So why not a duck quack?

OFFICER PILATO:
Nah, it looks like a false alarm.

ICE AGENT:
You mean you're gonna take his word for it.

OFFICER PILATO:
Whadda ya want me to do, torture him? I'm gonna call for back up. [*Exit*]

THOMAS:
We don't think he's a drug dealer, in fact we're sure he's not. What if he's really Jesus, who was supposed

to come back long ago? What makes you so sure he's not?

ICE AGENT:

Even if he is – I'm not saying that he is – but even if he is, what good is his being here now? He already gave his message thousands of years ago, and they – the Catlick Church, that is – are the only ones who understand it. Just look around you. Jesus said the truth will make you free. Well, there's a lot of truth around and a lot of untruth, and nobody except them knows the difference. Do you think humanity is ready for freedom, to be free? Don't make me laugh, he says. Humanity needs us and our Church to tell them what to do.

THOMAS:

But that's ...

ICE AGENT:

This isn't the first time he's come back, they taught him a lesson once – during the Middle Ages – and they'll teach him one again.

MAGDALENA:

[*To THOMAS, stepping between them*] What's that red mark on your cheek?

THOMAS:

[*Touches his cheek*] It's where he kissed me.

MAGDALENA:

HeyZeus?

THOMAS:

Yeah, it comes and goes.

MAGDALENA:

Wow! It looks like ...

THOMAS:

I almost forgot about it. What does it look like?

MAGDALENA:

[*Coming close*] It looks like a red hook. Did you cut yourself shaving?

OFFICER PILATO:

[*Enters holding rifle*] The SWAT guys'll be here in a few minutes.

ICE AGENT:

[*To OFFICER PILATO*] I bet that duck quack was their signal.

[*Lights dim until it's almost dark*]

OFFICER PILATO:

Hey, what's goin' on?

ICE AGENT:

It's an eclipse, stupid, there's an eclipse of the sun today. Be careful, he's coming. We can't wait for SWAT.

OFFICER PILATO:

Shit. [*Puts on eyeglasses*] My eyesight is bad enough.

Now all I need is a fucking eclipse. Is he armed?

ICE AGENT:

Yes, it looks like an AK-47 assault rifle. He's almost here. See that tree? [*Points*]

OFFICER PILATO:

The fig tree?

ICE AGENT:

Yeah.

OFFICER PILATO:

Yeah, I see it.

ICE AGENT:

He's right under it. You can't miss.

[*OFFICER PILATO kneels down in shooting position, aims ...*

THOMAS and MAGDALENA:

No! Don't shoot! He's not armed!

[*Three Loud drum beats correspond to gun shots*]

OFFICER PILATO:

Did I get him?

[*THOMAS and MAGDALENA run off in the direction of the fig tree*]

ICE AGENT:
Yes, my son. God bless you.

[BLACKOUT]

SCENE TWO

A SPECIAL LOVE

Setting: Prospect Park.

THOMAS:

[To the audience]

That's it. Do you see the problem? I can't expect even you, whose humble patience is prayed, to suspend disbelief – no, not even you can I expect to believe my story. You heard Bishop Casey: it's not convincing. What would I think if someone told me what I've told you? I'd be skeptical. I might even laugh. There were no witnesses. A kingdom for a witness. The disbelief of others has planted the seeds of doubt in my own mind – very fertile soil. I suppose that man is born to doubt. Without doubt, after all, there'd be no belief. Doubt and faith belong together like a couple in love, or a pair of ducks in the lake. If only it were otherwise.

I come here every once in a while, in the hope that he'll appear again – but he hasn't, yet. And the world seems more screwed up than ever. I came today because, well, I guess it was a dream. In it I received a message from a pigeon that I should go to the park, so I did. [*Sits on bench.*] You know that actually there was a witness, sort of: Magdalena. Wasn't she great? Although she didn't witness the walking on the lake part. But you know, in the meanwhile I've been studying something called Anthroposophy, which is a teaching by an Austrian guy named Rudolf Steiner. Problem is he died a hundred years ago, so all there is, are books he wrote and the many lectures he gave. He was an initiate, a "Christian Rosicrucian" one. No time to go into what that means now. I'm not sure I know myself anyway. He claimed that the Christ Jesus only came once ... physically that is. That the second coming means something else than physical. It means He may come to anyone or everyone, individually, spiritually. Everyone who wants him, that is, I guess.

So where does that leave HeyZeus? Aye, there's the rub. Was he or wasn't he the One? We'll probably never know, because he's dead. After he was shot dead by that cop, they said he was an illegal immigrant terrorist and scraped him off the ground and dumped him somewhere.

But even if HeyZeus wasn't "the One" returned, physically, maybe he was a kind of emissary sent here, to Earth that is, to try and instill some love and kindness in men's minds (women's too of course) if only he could survive a while before getting bumped off. But few people heard and saw him, like Magdalena. Wasn't she great? I really liked her a lot. Things are getting worse, because they don't let the good people who could work a change from evil to good live long enough.

[*Someone from the audience calls out: Who's they?*]

Hmm, yeah, good question, better than you think,

wise guy. There are two kinds of "they" – those who got whacked and the those who done it. Let's start with John F. Kennedy, Robert F. Kennedy and Martin Luther King Jr., all murdered during the same decade. I could go back in history and out into a wider geopolitical range. There were plenty of others, but those three are the ones I'm most familiar with. JFK had to go because he wanted to do things – and did some of them – that the top guns in the CIA and the FBI and the military didn't like at all, not at all.

[*Someone in the audience calls out: Like what?*]

Like getting out of Vietnam, a war he said we couldn't win. Like making peace with Cuba. Like making a deal with the Soviet Union (remember them?) when they installed nuclear rockets in Cuba, instead of invading that (still) poor country. So Khrushchev agreed and nuclear war was avoided. Evidence that "they" had him killed is provided by a half a dozen books available to everyone.

There's no real evidence though – that I know of – that RFK and MLK were rubbed out from inside. But there is more than one way to accomplish that. Rudolf Steiner was rubbed out that way. The Roman Catholic Church in the Catholic district of Switzerland developed a hate campaign so vicious that the anonymous faithful thought they were doing God's will by first destroying Steiner's monumental wooden Goetheanum by fire, then Steiner himself by poison. RFK who promised to end the Vietnam war; and MLK who demanded equality for all races and an end to the Vietnam war, and all war, could also have been rubbed out that way, by people who considered themselves saviors of America and the white race.

God knows what's going to happen now that an evil maniac like Donald Trump has been elected by a majority of voting citizens of the United States of America. Steiner prophesied that Ahriman – his name for the devil – will incarnate in the third millennium. I don't know if Trump is the devil, but if anyone alive now could fit the bill, it's him. But HeyZeus is dead, just when we need him most.

[*MAGDALENA enters with normal hair and clothes*]

THOMAS:

Magdalena! Wow! You look great.

MAGDALENA:

Thanks for not mentioning my hair and clothes.

THOMAS:

Where've you been? I missed you.

MAGDALENA:

[*Ignoring the question*] I have a message for you.

THOMAS:

You do? From who?

MAGDALENA:

From HeyZeus.

THOMAS:

Oh my God! I was afraid you'd say that. I mean ... he's like ... dead.

MAGDALENA:

Physically yes.

THOMAS:

What other way is there?

MAGDALENA:

Good point: Usually none. Don't you see, Tommy. I hope you don't mind me calling you that. You seem much more like a Tommy than a Thomas.

THOMAS:

No problem, Magda. What don't I see?

MAGDALENA:

Well, just because his body is dead doesn't mean *he* is.

THOMAS:

Don't tell me you can speak to dead people.

MAGDALENA:

No, but I can speak, or listen to, live souls.

THOMAS:

Gotcha! So, what's the message?

MAGDALENA:

Well, Tommy, if you're not gonna believe it, why should I tell you?

THOMAS:

Who said I'm not gonna believe it? I haven't even heard it yet, for god's sake.

MAGDALENA:

Your attitude. Well, I told HeyZeus I'd deliver it, so here goes. [*Long pause*]

THOMAS:

I'm waiting, with my best attitude.

MAGDALENA:

You are disappointed that HeyZeus is dead – as are the others who knew him – because you expected him to solve everything that's ...

THOMAS:

Not exactly.

MAGDALENA:

Or tell you what to do then. But times have changed since the Christ Jesus came to Earth and the gods, spiritual beings that is, were in charge and humans had to develop to freedom, whether we wanted to or not.

THOMAS:

That was a long time ago.

MAGDALENA:

Yeah, and in our fucking things up royally ...

THOMAS:

[*Interrupting*] Worse than ever.

MAGDALENA:

You can say that again.

THOMAS:

Worse than ever.

MAGDALENA:

Thanks. May I go on?

THOMAS:

Yes, sorry, please do.

MAGDALENA:

It means that we can't just pray to God or to Jesus to do something. We have to do it ourselves.

THOMAS:

OK, but how?

MAGDALENA:

Love each other as I have loved you.

THOMAS:

Jesus said that didn't he?

MAGDALENA:

Yes, and that's the message from HeyZeus.

THOMAS:

Should I love Trump?

MAGDALENA:

Don't be a wise ass. Anyway, Jesus said that to his disciples.

THOMAS:

How about if I start with you?

MAGDALENA:

I thought you'd never think of it.

THOMAS:

I love you, Magdalena.

MAGDALENA:

And I love you back, Tommy. [*They embrace*]

THOMAS:

Love your neighbor as yourself, I think he also said somewhere. But …

MAGDALENA:

But ours will be a special kind of love. Is that what you were going to say?

THOMAS:

It is. Can you read my mind?

MAGDALENA:

No, only your heart.

[*She takes his arm, and they exit together*]

END

MUSICAL SUGGESTIONS

The music accompanying this drama should reflect its themes of mystery, spirituality, societal tension, and emotional introspection. Here are some suggestions:

1. **Opening Scene (Prospect Park)**: Use soft, atmospheric instrumental music with a hint of mystery, such as piano or strings, to set the tone for Thomas' encounter with HeyZeus.
2. **HeyZeus' Appearance**: Incorporate uplifting yet enigmatic music, like a gospel-inspired melody or ethereal choral harmonies, to emphasize the spiritual and extraordinary nature of the moment.
3. **The Wake**: Play somber, reflective music, such as slow violin or cello pieces, to match the mood of grief and nostalgia.
4. **The Girlfriend (Judy)**: Use jazzy or soulful tunes to reflect Judy's vibrant personality and her emotional exchanges with Thomas.
5. **The Shrink**: Add subtle, minimalist background music, like soft piano or ambient sounds, to highlight the introspective and analytical tone of the scene.
6. **True Advertising**: Use upbeat, corporate-style music with a satirical edge to underscore the fast-paced, morally ambiguous world of advertising.
7. **The Bishop**: Incorporate traditional church music, such as organ or Gregorian chants, to contrast with the bishop's dismissive attitude.
8. **Prospect Park Redux**: Return to atmospheric music, with darker undertones, to reflect the tension and eventual tragedy of HeyZeus' fate.
9. **A Special Love**: End with a hopeful and tender melody, such as acoustic guitar or piano, to symbolize Thomas and Magdalena's embrace of love and humanity.

Additionally, the recurring use of "Let It Be" by The Beatles, as hummed by HeyZeus, could serve as a poignant motif throughout the drama, tying together its spiritual and emotional themes.

ON-LINE ACTIVITIES

Between the years 1910 and 1913, Rudolf Steiner wrote four Mystery Drama, or Mystery Plays. All four are online and are free to read and study by any interested soul. These links, along with contact links, are below.

Rudolf Steiner's Mystery Dramas: Overview
https://RudolfSteinereLib.org/Books/GA014/

The Portal of Initiation (Bn 14.1)
https://go.elib.com/MysDrama1

The Soul's Probation (Bn 14.2)
https://go.elib.com/MysDrama2

The Guardian of the Threshold (Bn 14.3)
https://go.elib.com/MysDrama3

The Souls' Awakening (Bn 14.4)
https://go.elib.com/MysDrama4

Adolf Arenson's Music for Rudolf Steiner's Mystery Dramas
https://go.elib.com/XflxL

Contacting the Publisher:
https://www.eLib.com/eMail/AnthroPubs/

Anthroposophical Publications website:
https://AnthroposophicalPublications.org/

Southern Cross Review:
https://SouthernCrossReview.org/

For permission to produce this play, contact the author at
fts@SouthernCrossReview.org

About The Playwright

Frank Thomas Smith

Frank Thomas Smith is an American expatriot who has lived most of his life in Europe (Switzerland and Germany) and South America (Argentina). During his career in the airline industry, he moonlighted in education (Waldorf), translating and writing — including children's fiction. What was once moonlighting is now full-time. He lives on a mountain in Argentina.

OTHER BOOKS
By **Frank Thomas Smith**
All titles available at your favorite Bookstore

A STREETCAR NAMED KARMA: Anthroposophy, also known as Spiritual or Esoteric Science, is not known for fantastic literature, nor fiction at all. So how can a story with a title like "A Streetcar Named Karma" qualify as anthroposophical? It does not ... until now. Therefore, this little book is groundbreaking. You may smile at times, even giggle or laugh; it may cause a lump in your throat, perhaps even a tear or two. This title is a part of the "Anthroposophical Fantasies" series of short stories, thirteen in all.

ISBN: 979-8361303991

LIFE ON MARS: Pool Hall buddies discover one of their bunch is harboring a visitor from Mars ... huh? And they try to enlist the help of Saul Bellow? Read this short story to find out what happens. A part of the *Anthroposophical Fantasies* series.

ISBN: 979-8361318759

THE PURLOINED POEM: How does one explain publishing someone else's work? What could possibly be a valid reason? How about reincarnation? Read this short story to find out about Peter Product's fate. A part of the Anthroposophical Fantasies series of short stories.

ISBN: 979-8361475056

THE GIRL IN THE FLOPPY HAT: Chance meetings can be an emotional whirlwind for some people, and this was no exception. The girl in the floppy hat and long dress was captivatingly wonderful, and almost too good to be true. Is she the one? Read this short story to find the answer. A part of the *Anthroposophical Fantasies* series of short stories.

ISBN: 979-8361331802

THE SPELL [sic erat scriptum]: Teaching at a school in a favela, or slum, in Brazil is no easy task, but when black magic enters the picture, things get out of hand ... especially when it involves your own children. A part of the *Anthroposophical Fantasies* series of short stories.

ISBN: 979 8861329576

A MULTICOLORED GODDESS IN ANTHROPOSOPHICAL HEAVEN: If you are an Argentine housewife interested in anthroposophy and your husband – who looks like Cary Grant – disappears, you would of course want to k now what happened to him. Based on a tip, you might even go to Italy, where Sofia Loren happens to reside. To make a long story short, you find him, or someone identical, but he's not really your husband. Actually, he's from a different universe and he's hanging out with Sofia Loren and... oh just read it and find out, if you think you can take it.

ISBN: 979-8361475056

TOTO THE FOURTH / TOTO CUARTO: Little "Wizard of Oz" white dogs named Toto must be a dime a dozen. That may be true for some folks, but for Frank, all he was interested in was four. The ocean waves brought back fond memories. Could they be telling him about his life's current events? Read all about it in this intriguing tale of love spanning the decades. A bilingual book.

ISBN: 979-8304567282

LOVE IN THE LIFE OF SPIES is, as its title suggests, a love story between two spies during the Cold War, an East German woman and an American man, each working for their respective opposing clandestine agencies and, therefore, against each other. Their meetings, seemingly accidental, unfold over years in the United States, Germany, Argentina, Paraguay and, finally, serve only to reveal an uncertain future. It asks the question: is such a love viable under such complicated and adverse geopolitical circumstances? Or was it meant to be – at least as a possibility – according to karma's blueprint. The answer, although not definitive, is maybe, or even yes involving, strangely enough, Anthroposophy.

ISBN: 978-1948302517

THE ROMAN CATHOLOC CHURCH / LA IGLESIA CATÓLICA ROMANA: In the Spring of 1920 Rudolf Steiner gave three lectures highly critical of the Roman Catholic Church's political history. The lectures were meant for members of the Anthroposophical Society only, but were soon leaked beyond the Society, resulting in some very bad feelings and even violence in the heavily Catholic Swiss district where Dornach is located. The lectures were transcribed from stenographic notes into German and are included in a series of seventeen lectures entitled: *Heilfaktoren für den Sozialen Organismus* (*Means for Healing the Social Organism*). This book contains English and Spanish translations of these three lectures.

ISBN: 978-1948302685

www.ingramcontent.com/pod-product-compliance
Lightning Source LLC
LaVergne TN
LVHW020934090426
835512LV00020B/3346